WE ARE PART OF THIS PLACE

BY LORRAINE SINTETOS

PEARSON
Scott
Foresman

Editorial Offices: Glenview, Illinois • Parsippany, New Jersey • New York, New York

Sales Offices: Needham, Massachusetts • Duluth, Georgia • Glenview, Illinois
Coppell, Texas • Sacramento, California • Mesa, Arizona

What is a citizen?

"He is a United States **citizen**." "Be a good citizen." Have you ever heard anyone say this? What does it mean?

A citizen is a member of a **community**. A community is a place where people live, work, and have fun together.

Being a Citizen

Being a citizen means you have certain rights in that country. You share in its **customs**. A custom is a way of doing things.

Responsibilities

In the United States we choose our leaders by voting. When a person becomes eighteen years old, he or she can vote.

When you vote, you have responsibilities. A responsibility is something we need to do.

We have a responsibility to pay taxes. The government uses tax money to take care of our needs.

We follow laws. Some laws keep us safe.
Other laws help us get along with each another.
    We want our country to be a good place
to live. That is why laws say you must go to
school. At school you learn to read, write, and
think. This helps you become a better citizen.

How do you become a citizen?

There are three ways to become a United States citizen.

The first way is to be born in the United States.

The second way is to have parents who are United States citizens.

The third way to become a citizen is to ask to become one. Some **immigrants** do this.

YOU MUST BE EIGHTEEN YEARS OLD OR OLDER.

YOU MUST HAVE LIVED IN THE UNITED STATES
FOR AT LEAST FIVE YEARS.

YOU MUST BE ABLE TO READ, SPEAK, AND WRITE ENGLISH.

YOU MUST KNOW ABOUT UNITED STATES HISTORY
AND GOVERNMENT.

★ ★ ★ ★ ★ ★ ★ ★ ★

This list tells how immigrants can become citizens.

An immigrant is a person who moves into a country to live there.

Some immigrants do not stay in the United States for very long. They go to school or work here and then go home. Others may stay to become citizens.

Immigrants must pass a test to become citizens. They must know about United States history and government.

You Can Be a Good Citizen.

Your community gives you a lot. You can ride its buses, visit its shops, go to its schools, and play in its parks.

Good citizens think about other people in their community.

Here are some ways to be a good citizen.

- Be fair.
- Be polite.
- Share what you have.
- Take turns.
- Solve problems by talking.

Your Community

Suppose you walk down a street and see trash everywhere. Would you like being there?

Trash makes us feel bad. Do not throw trash in the street. A clean community helps people feel good.

You are a world citizen too. You can keep Earth clean and beautiful.

How can you keep the air clean? Cars can make the air dirty. Ride your bike or walk when you can.

The Earth helps us meet our needs. We use trees to make paper. We use oil to drive our cars.

Take care of what you have. **Recycle** when you can. When we recycle, we use something again.

You Can Help.

Some citizens are volunteers. Volunteers help others. Volunteers work but they are not paid.

You can be a volunteer. You can visit older people. You can help children with their homework. Somewhere there is work you can do.

What You Can Do?

We want to be safe and happy. We want to enjoy our freedom.

You can do this by being a good citizen. Every good thing you do makes your community better. Every good thing you do makes the world better too.

Glossary

citizen a member of a community

community a place where people live, work, and have fun together

custom a way of doing things

immigrant a person who moves into a country to live there

recycle to use something again